Taking Tea with
Clarice Cliff

Taking Tea with Clarice Cliff

Leonard Griffin

Photography by
Michael Slaney & Leonard Griffin

PAVILION

Also by Leonard Griffin:

Clarice Cliff – the Bizarre Affair
(with Louis and Susan Pear Meisel)

The Rich Designs of Clarice Cliff
(with Richard Green and Des Jones)

to Daisy

This edition published in Great Britain in 1996 by
PAVILION BOOKS LIMITED
26 Upper Ground, London SE1 9PD
Text and illustrations copyright © Leonard Griffin 1996

The moral right of the author has been asserted
Text design by Cole design unit

A CIP catalogue record for this book is available from
the British Library

ISBN 1 85793 925 5

Typeset in Meridien with Futura by
Business Color Print, Welshpool, Powys, Wales
Printed and bound by Conti Tipocolor Florence, Italy

10 9 8 7 6 5 4 3 2 1

This book may be ordered by post direct from the
publisher. Please contact the Marketing Department.
But try your bookshop first.

Previous page: Crocus on a Stamford shape Early Morning set.

Contents

Clarice Cliff's *Bizarre* life

In 1930, when Clarice Cliff became Art Director of Newport Pottery, she achieved the distinction of being the first woman to reach such a high echelon in the Potteries (this and other terms are explained in the Glossary on p.117). She was, in effect, what we would nowadays call a 'career woman', but at the time when she was entrusted with the title Art Director by Colley Shorter, the factory's Victorian owner, society was dominated by men who could never have envisaged Clarice's rise to fame.

We can chronicle her phenomenal achievements, but it is still hard to appreciate them fully. She emerged as a major force in ceramic design between the Great Strike of 1926 and the Depression that began in 1930. Her most successful years mirror those of the serious financial depression that affected the whole world. Her prolific output of shapes and patterns has never since been equalled. With little formal artistic training, but a unique understanding of how to use colour and form, she emerged as Art Director of the factory group that pioneered modern design in ceramics in the Thirties. Clarice took both the design and the marketing of pottery to new heights.

Nothing in her childhood hinted at the distinguished career that was to follow. Like the majority of people from this industrial part of Staffordshire, she began life in a small two-up, two-down terraced house in Tunstall, with her parents and six brothers and sisters. The family was not poor but had a plain lifestyle.

Clarice seems to have been closer to her four sisters than to her two brothers. Her younger sister, Dorothy, was far more outgoing than Clarice. Known as Dolly, she loved dancing and shared a passion for dress-making with her sisters Hannah, Sarah and Ethel. All the Cliff girls were acknowledged by neighbours as being 'smart', but this related more to their ability to design their own frocks than to their income.

Clarice had a simple schooling, and spent much of each weekend with her sisters and friends at the services and Sunday School at Christchurch, in Tunstall. In the summer and at Easter they went on visits to the local countryside, where the children ran wild. A couple of times a year a dance in the church hall would cause great excitement, except for Clarice, who made it clear that she would far sooner be doing something constructive.

As was the case with virtually every working-class child at this time, Clarice had to leave school at thirteen and had little option but to work at a local potbank. Like all apprentices, she initially learned gilding and banding ware, but something fired her to look beyond working just to earn a living. She switched jobs twice and in 1916 arrived for her first day at A. J. Wilkinson's works at Newport in Burslem. It meant a long journey to work by tram and then having to walk, but it was a key factor in improving herself.

A. J. Wilkinson's was a successful potbank, which had

been owned by the Shorter family since 1894. A sprawling dark mass of bottle-ovens, kilns and production shops, it ran alongside the Trent-Mersey canal, which served to deliver the raw ingredients for the earthenware and the coal to fire it. Nearly 400 workers were employed and every stage of production was manual. They negotiated steep wooden stairs or piles of coal while carrying on their shoulders long boards covered in ware. They certainly never dropped the boards – it would have cost them their job. In the distance they could see fields around the factory, but nearby these were scarred by a huge white shard ruck: broken pieces of ware spreading over many acres.

Wilkinson's was run by Colley Shorter and his brother Guy. Colley was a wealthy, Victorian, upper-class man with a taste for fine furnishings and antiques that complemented his Arts and Crafts home. He would have had no idea who Clarice was when she joined. Indeed, it would have been unlikely that he would ever have had occasion to address her. No one could have predicted her rise to become Art Director of Newport Pottery.

Her fellow-workers recall that while Clarice was friendly, rather than socializing she preferred wandering around the factory learning about the various processes by asking and looking. Each job required particular skills. Plates and saucers were pressed from solid clay by flat-pressers. Teapots and other vessels were made by pouring slip into moulds; once dry the piece was carefully removed and sent for firing. Most of the workers had no

A stunning collection of Clarice Cliff's *Stamford, Bon Jour* and *Conical* teapots, showing the reverse of the design.

The front of the *Stamford, Bon Jour* and *Conical* teapots.
Top row: *Appliqué Windmill, Summerhouse, Rudyard.*
Middle row: *Red Roofs, Appliqué Lucerne Orange, Carpet.*
Bottom row: *Crocus, Appliqué Lugano Orange, Sunray.*

interest in the coal-fired bottle-ovens, but Clarice would watch as the heavy saggars full of pots were piled thirty feet high by labourers using ladders. One saggar would hold anything from twenty-four to forty-two teapots. Clarice even went to the clay end (the worst part of the factory in which to work) and befriended a young boy called Reg Lamb, who secretively purloined expensive modelling clays for her. As her confidence grew, she persuaded the oven firemen and placers to fire her pieces. When her fellow-workers had lunch outdoors, Clarice stayed at her bench modelling figures.

Her independence led to her being noticed by the works manager, who reported to Colley Shorter that she showed promise. By 1922 she was given an apprenticeship as a modeller and assigned to work with two elderly designers at Wilkinson's, John Butler and Fred Ridgway. As well as modelling, Clarice was entrusted with decorating their prestigious art pottery. These pieces were designed for exhibitions, to attract buyers to the company's stand and encourage sales of the more everyday fancies and tableware. Her new role was significant, as she had escaped from the artistic strait-jacket of being just a paintress, and now had the chance to make her own mark.

Working in the design studio gave Clarice the time and facilities to pursue her true love of modelling. By 1926 several of her rather naïve figurines were added to the factory's range, including a cartoon-style duckling, who preceded Donald Duck by several years. This was later adapted to become the handle of an egg-cup set. A more graceful figurine of a girl holding aloft a candle sconce, modelled as a flower posy, was produced for over ten years. However, as much as Clarice aspired to be a modeller, fate intervened and provided her true vocation.

Wilkinson's had bought the Newport Pottery that adjoined its factory in 1920, inheriting another 300 workers and a large warehouse full of traditionally shaped ware. The pieces were of poor quality and unsaleable, but in 1927 Clarice had the idea of covering them in bold colours to hide their defects. Surprisingly, Colley mellowed quickly to the enthusiasm of his first female designer and she was given her own studio at Newport. With the help of a young paintress, Gladys Scarlett, Clarice now developed her own ideas. She found that simple designs of triangles could be executed speedily, and with banding added to cover the rest of the body, faults were well hidden.

In spring 1927 Clarice left Gladys producing these trial pieces while she was sent to the prestigious Royal College of Art, in London's Kensington. Her fees were paid by Colley, who saw this as a way of refining her innate ability. However, it was not the time she spent modelling clay under the guidance of sculptor Gilbert Ledward that was to advance her talent, but her forays into London's galleries and shops. Here she encountered for the first time a mass of paintings, silver and glass that opened her mind to a whole new direction for ceramic design.

While any of the major Stoke-on-Trent Potteries could

Designed before Clarice was Art Director, the traditional *Globe* shape teapot is shown here in *Original Bizarre* from 1928, and in *Trees & House*, which was issued from 1930 to 1933.

One of the first *Conical* shape
Early Morning sets in the very
simple *Desny* design from
1929.

have used this new Jazz Age style, their designers preferred to cling to conservative shapes and designs. Stoke had not initially responded to the outpouring of creative artistic ideas focused at the 1925 Exposition des Arts Décoratifs et Industriels in Paris. The Art Deco exhibition (as it was eventually named) was to influence all Thirties' design in Britain, from furniture to cinemas, from carpets to fashion. It was Clarice Cliff, however, who first took its principles and instilled them into ceramics.

Clarice returned to Stoke-on-Trent a changed woman. The impetus of her visit led to long discussions with Colley in her studio, generally conducted over afternoon tea and behind closed doors. They may have done this to keep her ideas secret from other potteries (copying designs was a standard occurrence at the time) or, as factory staff observed, perhaps they wanted some privacy. In later years she talked of a brief visit to Paris at this time. It is inconceivable that she could have arranged or afforded this herself, and it later transpired that she had probably gone with Colley Shorter, which is why it was kept secret. This trip was clearly the catalyst for both her artistic and her personal growth.

Early in 1928 Clarice recruited more young hand-paintresses to execute designs on the old unsaleable stock, and when she chose the name *Bizarre* for this range she unknowingly started on a career that was to change ceramic history.

The initial *Bizarre* designs were crude triangles drawn

in brown or green, which were then enamelled in two or three colours. The ware had great impact because of its sheer simplicity – there was nothing like it being offered for sale by pottery retailers. The factory salesmen were sceptical about its appeal but knew it was wise to react positively to Shorter's enthusiasm for the ideas of the woman already perceived as his protégée. The most experienced salesman, Ewart Oakes, took a car-load to an Oxford dealer. To his surprise she bought it all, and suddenly the *Bizarre* ball was rolling. Clarice's hunch had been right!

Clarice wanted to enlarge the *Bizarre* range and found Colley agreeable to providing source material for her, so she compiled a library of books on flowers, contemporary painting, and sets of prints. The ideas she culled from these, mixed with her unusual taste for colour, swiftly accelerated the development of *Bizarre*, and the name was then used for all her designs.

Clarice's first floral pattern was to be her most successful. She experimented with painting *Crocus* flowers and found that the brush strokes exactly resembled the petals, while a few green lines for the leaves completed the effect. The pattern was immediately so successful that Ethel Barrow, the first paintress to produce it, had to teach whole teams of girls how to execute it. The design's popularity endured throughout Clarice's career.

Many of Clarice's girls were to find that life as a *Bizarre* paintress was more enjoyable than they had anticipated.

Clarice's earliest teapot was *Bones the Butcher,* which she designed in 1928, but which was credited as being by 'Joan Shorter Aged 8'. Later examples have just a Clarice Cliff *Bizarre* mark.

Clarice's 'signature' design *Crocus* on a *Stamford* shape *Early Morning set*. This popular combination of shape and design was produced from 1930 to 1936.

Late in 1928 Clarice and Colley organized a demonstration of hand-painting in the foyer of the Waring & Gillow store in London. This type of promotion was unusual for the time, as most companies limited their activities to static displays.

Colley Shorter had allowed John Butler and Fred Ridgway to be credited on wares earlier in the Twenties, but in Clarice Cliff he recognized a fresh concept in marketing. Linking a woman's name to pottery aimed primarily at women opened up new promotional horizons. Clarice's artistic naïveté and charismatic personality magnetically captured the attention of the public and the press.

The Waring & Gillow demonstration was probably the first *and* last time that Clarice did hand-painting in public herself. She sat with three of her paintresses for the press pictures, but as soon as they were taken she left with Colley. He realized that her value lay in being a figurehead and it did not really matter who was painting the ware, as long as the public could see it being done. Naturally, the young paintresses were more interested in Clarice and Colley going off together than in their demonstration. When they returned to the Potteries all the other girls in the *Bizarre* shop heard about it.

Soon there were twenty paintresses doing Clarice's designs, and a special painting shop was set up on the top floor of an old three-storey building overlooking the canal. Wooden benches were installed, where the girls worked for five and a half days a week for a wage of just

A *Stamford* shape trio in the 1930 *Fantasque Melon* design features part of the pattern, the full design being shown radially on the plate behind.

six shillings. Shelves by the girls' benches held boards full of decorated ware, which was carried across the site to the enamel kiln for final firing. Workers referred to Clarice's decorating shop as the *Bizarre* shop, and the paintresses who were briefly the *Bizarre* 'babes' became known as the *Bizarre* 'girls', a name they still use more than sixty years later. Too busy to train and supervise them herself now, Clarice employed Lily Slater as the 'missus' for her growing team.

All *Bizarre* ware was hand-painted using enamels mixed from powder colour, turps and fat-oil. The younger apprentices ground the paints for the more experienced decorators. These were then applied on-glaze, which enabled a larger range of brighter colours to be used than the under-glaze process. As they learned the skills of hand-painting, the decorators specialized in one particular part of the process. The outliners drew the silhouette of the design in one colour, then enamellers added the individual colours between these. Finally, a bander & liner added colourful bands around the ware by placing it on a rotating potter's wheel and skilfully applying the brush. Banding colours varied between patterns and were a distinctive frame that gave *Bizarre* an individual style.

During 1929 Clarice's simple triangles evolved into motifs such as *Sunray* and *Umbrellas & Rain,* which captured the Art Deco spirit. Some of these appeared under a separate range name, *Fantasque,* which was developed into a major part of Clarice's output. The most outrageous new line was *Delecia*, ware drenched in dripping enamels that ran all over it like a colourful storm. Elsie Nixon, the first paintress to do this, usually ended up covered in more paint than the pottery! Elsie also assisted in developing the *Bizarre* advertising photographs that Clarice took in her own studio. Ironically, most of the publicity for Clarice's colourful wares was limited to black and white reproduction.

Clarice's new patterns looked incongruous on the traditional shapes, so she complemented them with her first major range of shapes, inspired by and named after *Conical* forms. A series of bowls with triangular feet were produced after she insisted to the sceptical staff that they were technically feasible. By September she had issued the stylish *Conical* teaware range. The teapot had a solid triangular handle, as did the cups. Triangular feet were also used for the milk jug and sugar basin. Technically these pieces were of high quality, and were covered in a more refined glaze than usual. The factory called this honeyglaze, and it provided a warm background for Clarice's colour combinations and designs.

Unlike anything else available in the shops, these shapes proved instantly popular with young buyers. It became fashionable to give *Conical* sets as engagement or wedding presents. In London, Birmingham, Manchester and many other cities shop windows were full of immensely colourful displays of *Early Morning* sets, and this allowed the factory to employ yet more decorators.

In 1929 the growing team of *Bizarre* girls was joined by

One of the few *Bizarre* girls who was a close friend of Clarice was Clara Thomas, who is shown demonstrating banding at an exhibition of *Bizarre* hand-painting in London in 1929.

four boys aged between fourteen and fifteen. Apprenticed as designers, they spent most of their time executing the outlines for Clarice's patterns. On the few occasions when they were allowed to do original work, anything that Clarice thought good enough to be issued always appeared with her backstamp!

Bizarre painting demonstrations in stores around Britain increased that year. The girls were thrilled to do them, as most had never travelled outside the Potteries. Mindful of their parents' concerns about them being away from home for the first time, Clarice ensured that they were found suitable accommodation where they would be chaperoned. She took them to Stoke-on-Trent station, gave them money for their trip and waved them off. The four boys were not used for hand-painting demonstrations, as Clarice thought that the girls better fitted the image of pottery painted 'by a woman for women'. She did not perhaps realize it, but the girls were becoming her family. She was devoting her life to her work and setting the mould for a term that was not to appear for several decades – 'career woman'.

Until this time Clarice's designs had been dominated by bold geometrics and all-over abstracts and florals. However, some simple landscapes began to appear. These were typified by *Trees & House,* a simple but classic pattern with a cottage nestling among stylized trees and bushes. It was produced in several colourways from late 1929 to 1933. Clarice added numerous variations on this landscape theme to her range these are now appreciated

The colourful 'runnings' of
the 1930 *Delecia* pattern on a
Conical shape *Early Morning set.*

One of the most popular designs on Clarice's *Stamford* shape *Early Morning set* was *Fantasque Trees & House*, which was produced from 1930 to 1933.

as a very British expression of Art Deco and are some of her most sought-after patterns.

One of Clarice's first girls was Cissy Rhodes, who recalled how quickly things changed.

We used to do lots of patterns and fresh things at the time. When 'Miss Cliff' designed a new pattern she would want someone to try it out, and I would do samples for her. Latona Red Roses *was very difficult to do – you had to put the paint on very thickly. And I did some* Appliqué *landscapes and* Age of Jazz *figures.*

Clarice treasured two folios of prints by a French artist called Edouard Benedictus whose work she particularly admired, and from him she found colour. His brilliantly executed, vividly coloured *pochoir* prints inspired more than just a few of her designs. His brave use of colour was something she took to heart, and *Bizarre* took on new hues during the following months. A brighter red, called coral, was introduced, together with a strident blue and a whole range of new shades. These colours had previously been limited to the factory's art pottery, because of their cost, but Clarice used them liberally for everyday teasets, vases and fancies.

It was not just Clarice's palette that was changing. She could now afford to buy good-quality clothes. The handmade frocks that she and her sisters had diligently sewn out of necessity were replaced with a more fashionable selection from the department stores she visited while promoting *Bizarre*. Sensibly, as she had a full, rounded figure, she chose dark colours such as blue georgette and black crêpe de Chine. She accessorized these with smart black shoes and topped her outfit with a cloche hat and a Liberty scarf.

As Clarice prospered, so did the girls. Unlike many other workers in the Potteries in the Thirties, they were never laid off. It was customary to give much of their earnings to their parents, but they still had enough left to enjoy a good social life, and their friends noticed that they became more smartly dressed. This probably had more impact on people in the Potteries than the fact that Clarice's name was stamped on the 1,500 dozen pieces of *Bizarre* that the factory was producing each week.

The opposite was true in the South of England, the biggest market for *Bizarre*, where the public began to ask, 'Who is Clarice Cliff?' Colley Shorter decided to let them find out. Gradually, under his guidance, Clarice learnt to meet the women whose tastes she was so accurately able to assess. Advertisements in national newspapers, illustrated with pictures of Clarice holding a *Bizarre* vase, proclaimed: 'Come to Lawleys and meet Miss Clarice Cliff.'

Clarice quickly inherited Colley Shorter's promotional flair. For trade shows and exhibitions she devised original and eye-catching displays. An Art Deco tiered circular stand that was ideal for displaying her modern shapes was produced (and patented). Promotional bowls had her *Bizarre by Clarice Cliff* logo hand-painted on them, and several of her vases were made in extra-large sizes just for display at exhibitions. She would often spend two or three days setting up the stands with the help of her newly recruited assistant, Hilda Lovatt, who was also to become a lifelong friend. Together they ensured that every display was perfect, and filled *Bizarre* vases with fresh flowers just before the show opened. Her competitors started to take note.

Bizarre ware was now attracting orders from overseas. Colley Shorter had developed a good network of dealerships in most Commonwealth countries during the Twenties, and the larger profit-margins made it a good line to export. Consignments of ware went twice yearly to major stores in Australia, New Zealand, South Africa and South America. Often sample pieces were originated for these countries and were not sold elsewhere. This left a legacy of rare designs, some of which still await discovery.

When Clarice was promoted to Art Director of Newport Pottery in 1930 it was noted in the press that she was the first woman in the Potteries to hold this prestigious role. It was around this time that she left the family home in Tunstall and moved to Snow Hill, in Hanley. Her flat was situated over a hairdresser's salon, and consisted of a lounge, bedroom, bathroom and small kitchen with a dining area. While Colley was known to visit Clarice regularly, factory colleagues were rarely invited: her responsibilities at the factory dictated that few of her workers could be friends. An exception was Eric Grindley, an office boy whom Clarice paid to do odd jobs. Eric came from a conventional suburban home and recalled that Clarice's décor was as *Bizarre* as her pottery.

The lounge contained a large black and white mottled marble fireplace with unusual Chinese brass fire-irons. The chimney breast and adjoining wall were decorated with a striking hand-painted mural in orange, red, blue, black and green, which depicted what could only be described as a Bizarre *forest scene with huge leaves, and lotus flowers and fruits. The wall was papered in a bright red paper with big scrolled motifs, the doors were painted in vivid red, with panels picked out with black. The walls were adorned with 'Picasso'-type pictures. Vases and lamp bases were Clarice Cliff's own shapes, banded in orange and black, colours that matched a Chinese-type carpet. The lounge furniture was of Regency type, dark wood with upholstery of red and gold brocade. There was an occasional table in mahogany and glass, and an antique cabinet almost the length of one wall.*

The *Bizarre* combination of Clarice's mural with an antique cabinet suggests that the flat was a joint effort by Clarice and Colley. The furniture had been provided by Benny Jacobs, a local antiques dealer who was a friend of Colley. Colley had also ensured Clarice's independence by having his chauffeur teach her to drive, and by this time she had a small car. The gossip about Clarice and Colley was further fuelled.

Clarice had little time to enjoy her flat, apart from weekends, as her days at Newport Pottery were long. Despite the public's positive response, sales during the Depression were never easy. Her answer was to produce more and more shapes and designs. In September 1930

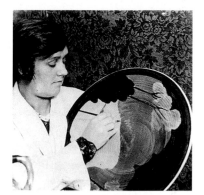

A press picture of Clarice supposedly decorating an *Appliqué Etna* charger. In reality she did her designs in water-colour and her decorators then executed them on the pottery.

she issued what was probably to become her most significant teaset, the *Stamford*. Its very English name belied its origins, as it was originally designed by the French silversmiths Tétard Frères. Its flat sides were ideal for *Bizarre* designs, as different parts of the pattern could appear on each side. The *Stamford* shape was launched at the First Avenue Hotel in London, initially in *Trees & House*, *Melon* and *Crocus*. The eye-catching shapes proved popular and customers soon ordered the ware in many of Clarice's designs, including *Carpet* and *Tennis*.

At the same exhibition Clarice unveiled her most esoteric ceramic creation, the five *Age of Jazz* figures. Three of these featured couples, the women in ballgowns, their partners in evening dress, dancing cheek-to-cheek. Two further figures provided the music, one a banjo and piano player, the other a saxophonist and drummer, painted in vivid red and black. Mounted on ceramic bases, they were flat-sided, so that the woman's ballgown could be seen on one side and the man's trousers on the other. Intended as table decorations for meals or while listening to the wireless, the figures proved a clever marketing ploy and attracted a great deal of publicity in the national press. Posed pictures of Clarice 'painting' them headed coverage of the exhibition, but – as she and Colley had anticipated – it was the *Stamford* teaware that attracted orders.

Perhaps stimulated by the interest in the *Stamford*, Clarice produced another innovative teapot. Its tubular body had a square mortar-board-shaped lid and fittingly

A *Conical* shape teapot, the inside of a *Conical* sugar bowl and a plate in *Appliqué Lucerne Orange* from 1930.

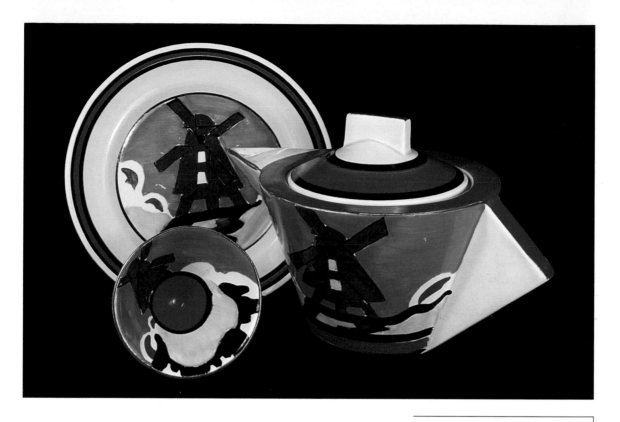

A *Conical* shape teapot, the inside of the sugar bowl and a plate in *Appliqué Windmill* from 1930.

she named it *Eton*. Clarice was either unable, or did not want, to develop a matching milk and sugar, so she teamed it with shapes from her *Conical* ware.

She was now exceptionally busy, but still looked after her girls and organized a *Bizarre* outing to Llangollen in Wales. They all met outside Burslem Town Hall, were given a box of sandwiches, slab-cake and lemonade and piled on to a charabanc, singing, laughing and talking all the way. 'Mr Colley' and 'Miss Cliff' followed behind in one of his cars. At Llangollen everyone bought a walking stick, and after their ramble Colley untypically lay down in the long grass in his suit. Clarice, who wore a stylish flapper's dress and a cloche hat, organized three-legged and egg-and-spoon race, perhaps remembering her own Sunday School outings. The younger girls enjoyed it thoroughly; the older ones felt they were 'back at school'. They ate their picnic in the sunshine, and the paintress Vera Hollins, who had a camera with her that day, took some pictures that some of the girls still treasure.

A *Stamford* shape teapot, milk and sugar in *Appliqué Red Tree* from 1930.

By the end of 1930 Clarice's wares were being sold from shops throughout Britain. In London she supplied Barker's, Selfridges, Waring & Gillow and even Harrod's, for which she produced a special design, *Doré*. The amazing success of a female designer was a novelty to the public, who became familiar with her name from further newspaper interviews. A *Bristol Times* reporter wrote, 'It was at a private exhibition now being held in London that I discovered Clarice Cliff. A brown-haired, vivacious,

A *Stamford* shape teapot, milk and sugar in *Appliqué Lugano Orange* from 1930.

Clarice Cliff on one of her rare days away from the factory when she took her girls to Llangollen for a works outing in the summer of 1930.

very alive-looking girl, she was presiding over a section of the exhibition which consisted of pottery she designed.'

Clarice explained how *Bizarre* had developed.

All the pottery for which I am responsible is hand-painted. At first I did all the work myself but since I started my work has grown tremendously. It would of course be impossible for me to do it all now, so I teach boys and girls who show aptitude for design my own methods. I have always loved bright colours, and think the modern idea of using these for pottery and china adds such a cheerful note to our tables and to our rooms.

The promotional highlight of 1931 was the *Bizooka*, a five-foot-high horse constructed of *Bizarre* ware. The concept had been created in a drawing used for a 1929 advertisement, but Clarice made it a reality with the help of the factory's technicians. It was designed not to be sold, but to sell the ware. It was loaned to retailers who displayed it in their windows alongside *Fantasque* and *Bizarre* ware.

Paintress Rene Dale joined in 1931 and recalls that the *Bizarre* girls had fun with the *Bizooka*. Many local firms contributed floats for the annual 'Crazy Day' parade to raise funds for hospitals. For the Newport Pottery float the girls dressed as jockeys and ran alongside the *Bizooka*. In London at the First Avenue Hotel it was the centre-piece of the stand and was photographed with well-known personalities hired by Colley Shorter to endorse *Bizarre*. These included the new world-land-speed record-holder Sir Malcolm Campbell and bandleader Jack Hilton.

Clarice's output of new landscapes was prolific in 1931, and the vibrant coral-red featured on both her new *Fantasque Summerhouse* and *Red Roofs* designs. Orders flooded in for these on her *Stamford* teaware, and Clarice took on extra paintresses, including her sister Ethel as a bander & liner, and outliner Sadie Maskrey, who recalled the daily routine.

We didn't have a tea break, except at lunch. There was a geyser which was always boiling, where you would make tea. We had to sneak snacks at the bench in the morning, take sandwiches for lunch, and one of the young girls was sent to fetch anything people wanted from town. She used to get fruit for Clarice, who never sat with us at lunchtime. She was never one of the girls. We occasionally used to go down to a little room at lunchtime and learn dancing; we used to sing and dance at the same time. Some days we would 'work over' until 7.30 p.m. to supplement our income.

Colley Shorter was a teapot devotee and encouraged Clarice to produce more new teaware shapes. Next came *Daffodil*, which was entirely original, had its own cups, milk and sugar, but was less Deco in style than the *Conical* or *Stamford* shapes.

By 1931 Clarice had sixty female decorators in her *Bizarre* shop, plus the four boys. They knew how fortunate they were to have work when nearly three million people in Britain were unemployed. Clarice

Colley Shorter relaxing on the *Bizarre* outing to Llangollen.

The 1931 *Fantasque Summerhouse* design on *Stamford* shape teaware, which interestingly has the summerhouse on the reverse of the teapot.

needed to be strong with them to maintain discipline, and she would walk through the shop several times a day to supervise, always taking time to guide a beginner or to reprimand any shoddy work. However, when she went away to London for trade shows things became rather more raucous, and the boys were known to chase round after the girls with dead mice. One of the boys bravely swung over the Trent-Mersey canal on a crane to impress the girls, but fell into the water and so lost half a day's wages.

Clarice's pottery continued to attract much attention and publicity. In December 1931 photographs of the production process covered the entire back page of the *Daily Sketch*. Colley Shorter's faith in Clarice a few years earlier was amply rewarded, as the headline read, 'How famous *Bizarre* ware is made at Stoke'.

Clarice had met the first B B C 'disc jockey' Christopher Stone at one of her London shows and was a radio devotee all her life. A local wireless dealer recalled her regularly taking in her accumulator for charging. When she introduced a radio into the *Bizarre* shop to help her decorators concentrate and to increase production it became a newspaper story. The *Bizarre* girls were pictured with the wireless and the caption read, 'These girl paintresses at the Newport Pottery works have musical interludes on the "wireless" to assist them at work. It is claimed that this original method of "working to music" has stopped talking at work and increased output by twenty-five percent.'

The rare *Eton* shape teapot in *Solitude* from 1932.

Never exhausted for new ideas, Clarice created floral designs for 1932, including *Nasturtium, Chintz,* and a major new landscape that was to sell well on *Stamford* teasets, *Orange Roof Cottage.* Her fascination with natural finishes led to *Delecia* being revived, this time as part of patterns of citrus fruit or flowers. These bright, gay patterns were produced both on *Conical* and *Stamford* teasets, but very few appeared on the *Daffodil* and *Eton* shapes.

Clarice perceived a change in the public taste during 1932, a demand for more pastel colours. She therefore issued her *Melon* design in a paler colourway, and launched a major new pattern called *Gibraltar.* A subtle symphony of pink, mauve, blue, yellow and green, it featured white-sailed yachts on a blue and yellow sea in front of the Rock. It was immediately popular on her *Stamford* teaware. Variations on the best-selling *Crocus* pattern in more pastel shades were to follow.

Clarice's paintresses began to appreciate that *Bizarre* was rather special, and the security of their work enabled them to enjoy life in a way that most people in the Potteries could not afford to at the time. Marjory Higginson would spend nine pence on the best seats at the opera, when it came to the Theatre Royal in Hanley; Annie Beresford favoured seeing Rudolph Valentino on the screen of the Coliseum or Palace in Burslem. Some of the girls were 'ladding', but the four boy decorators do not seem to have been the object of their attentions. The boys stayed together socially. At work, when they were not outlining, they hand-painted samples, modelled under Clarice's instruction, or decorated large exhibition pieces.

Clarice was never a purist designer, but explored all styles. In 1932, in contrast to her geometric shapes, she designed *Marguerite* teaware, which combined soft, flowing shapes with handles of modelled flowers on the teapot, cups and milk jug. But her commercial sense took a back seat when she enthusiastically developed a range based on ware modelled as tree boles. Decorated in mossy shades resembling bark, *Le Bon Dieu* was a commercial failure. Later examples were issued in floral designs to use the embarrassingly large stock of the shape in the glost warehouse.

If Clarice thought that events had completely changed her life in the preceding four years, she was in for a further shock. In a speech in 1932 the Prince of Wales challenged British industry to 'raise the standard of design in its products'. He believed that it was not innovative enough to compete with imports. The simultaneous publication of the Gorell committee's *Report on Art and Education* meant that many industries where design was essential were drawn into a single project linking them with well-known artists. With his factories' good reputation for their earthenware, Colley Shorter negotiated that production of the project's pieces would be done at Wilkinson's, under the supervision of Clarice Cliff.

Just before Christmas 1932 the girls were surprised when Santa Claus appeared in the *Bizarre* shop. It was

Colley Shorter disguised in a white beard and outfit, bearing a bag of gifts. He gave each girl a Bakelite powder bowl. This generous behaviour was untypical. What the girls did not realize was that the bowls had been taken by 'Santa' in part-payment of a debt!

The British Industries Fair was Clarice's first major trade show of 1933, and as usual was visited by the King and Queen. They were keen to support industry during the Depression and Queen Mary generally chose a few pieces of *Crocus* each year to add to her collection, although she seemed to avoid the bolder *Bizarre* designs. Clarice's newest pattern was *Windbells* and she was pictured in the press demonstrating to a bevy of her girls how it should be painted. This was ironic, since most of them were actually better paintresses than Clarice, whose work was not as precise. She had created another new teapot, an innovative shape that she called *Bon Jour.* Round but flat-sided, with a stylish pastille-shaped knob, it was a natural progression from the *Stamford. Bon Jour* looked stunning in Clarice's new 1933 landscapes, *Secrets, Rudyard* and *Honolulu,* and was also popular in *Crocus,* which by this time needed a team of twenty decorators to keep up with demand. *Bon Jour* quickly established itself as her most popular teapot and inspired a new line in tableware, *Biarritz.* This incorporated elements from a variety of her shapes: plates were square or oblong with a central round well; tureens were semi-circular, flat-sided with oblong lids.

When the Society of Industrial Artists issued a list of

A *Stamford* shape *Early Morning set* in *Carpet,* issued in 1930 and 1931.

designers for the project that she was to supervise, Clarice read through and noted the names of Vanessa Bell, John Armstrong, Dod Proctor and Paul Nash. Possibly she did not realize the immensity of the task ahead of her. She had to liaise with all the artists, whose brief was to produce innovative patterns for tableware, so she had little time to dedicate to her own work during 1933. Colley was glad for her to concentrate on the project, as he realized the tremendous prestige that the job held. With their life and work totally interwoven, he may also have seen the project as a way of giving Clarice the social credibility that her talents as a designer merited. He ensured that under the artist's name each piece bore the backstamp *'Produced in Bizarre by Clarice Cliff'*.

The Artists in Industry pieces débuted in the summer of 1933 at the British Industrial Art in Relation to the Home exhibition at Dorland Hall, London. A negative critical and public response forced a reappraisal. Colley Shorter was consulted on a further choice of artists and by 1934 nearly thirty had contributed. The names read like a *Who's Who* of British artists of the day, and now included Graham Sutherland, Duncan Grant, Frank Brangwyn, Barbara Hepworth, Ben Nicholson and Laura Knight. Socially Clarice had little in common with them, but in one she found a real soul-mate.

Laura Knight was as colourful a character as Clarice, and they had met once on a train before the project started. They shared an unorthodox approach to art. To

A *Stamford* shape trio in *Fantasque Red Roofs* from 1931 and 1932.

capture the colour of the circus for her oil paintings, Laura Knight had lived and toured with Carmo's Circus, and these works provided the inspiration for her own *Circus* tableware. This included modelled shapes, which appealed to Clarice as they were more refined versions of the figurines she herself had made in the Twenties. A candlestick was two chubby clowns back-to-back, and a tureen handle was a clown 'doing the splits'. The stylish teapot was a strange mixture of humour and traditional Potteries styling, being globe-shaped but with clown feet, an acrobat handle and other humorous touches.

Laura Knight's *Circus* ware was launched later in 1934. It was costly to produce; one of the few who could afford the complete set at £70 was Gracie Fields, who was then earning £40,000 for each film she made for Associated Talking Pictures.

The pressures of working on the project led to disagreements between Clarice and Colley, overheard by the girls. They found this surprising, as previously Clarice had always been 'the apple of his eye'. Their impression was that her heart was not in the project. Despite the government impetus behind it, and touring exhibitions in 1934, Artists in Industry was deemed a failure. *Bizarre* shapes without *Bizarre* patterns did not tempt the public to pay higher prices just because of the signature of a well-known artist on the back.

Colley Shorter generally spent his weekends at Chetwynd House, with his wife Annie and two daughters, when the factories finished at 12.30 p.m. on

Saturdays. This was one of the few times that Clarice had to enjoy her flat at Snow Hill, as she often worked late on weekday nights. Having to maintain a distance from her staff, she invited few of her girls round, although sometimes she served Saturday afternoon tea. She would invite her sister Ethel, Hilda Lovatt and Clara Thomas, one of her first paintresses, and they would chat while the wireless played in the background. Hilda recalled how on one occasion, in return for tea, she had helped Clarice decorate the bathroom ceiling with shiny yellow and black paper, and paint the walls black. This décor matched a *Bizarre* bathroom set that Clarice had banded in the same colours.

Occasionally Clarice would visit her parents at weekends. Paintress Rene Dale, whose cousin Nancy was the daughter of Clarice's sister Sarah, sometimes joined them at their Fuller Street home. After Clarice had left, Rene once slept in the bedroom that Clarice had shared with Ethel. She recalls that the ceiling was black with silver stars, and the furniture was black, apart from the drawers, which were bright orange. Clarice clearly loved to live *and* sleep with colour!

Shortly after the Artists in Industry project Clarice made a series of ware modelled to look as if it had been thrown on a potter's wheel. The shape was called *Lynton* and matching tea- and coffeeware was produced. Initially it sold well in Clarice's *Blue Firs* and *Coral Firs* landscapes, but it was also issued in a new coloured body called *Goldstone*, which was less successful.

Reverting to her first love of modelling, Clarice now produced *My Garden*. The vases from this set had modelled floral bases and smooth sides, and matching teaware was made. It débuted at the *Daily Mail* Ideal Home Exhibition in July 1934 and proved popular for the rest of the decade, numerous variations being issued annually. The ware garnered yet more coverage in newspapers and magazines, which mentioned 'Clarice Cliff, the only woman art director in the pottery trade'.

Clarice and Colley booked more 'stars' for their display at the Holborn Restaurant in 1934. These included Leslie Henson, Bobby Howes and members of the 'Crazy Gang'. The biggest star, though, was Gertrude Lawrence, an internationally known actress who had appeared with Noël Coward in the première of his *Private Lives* in 1930.

Late in 1934 the *Trieste* shape was added to Clarice's teaware range. The teapot, milk and sugar were triangular in profile, with a curved edge. Although the plates and saucers were the same shape, *Conical* cups were used. The market for unusual teaware shrank at this time so the well-conceived shape was only issued in small quantities and is now found in just a few designs in muted colours.

The year of 1935 was one of change. King George V celebrated his Silver Jubilee, and in August the unemployment level fell below two million for the first time since 1930. Some of Clarice's male outliners left at this time, but the sixty remaining decorators had a new 'missus' to supervise them. Alice Andrews had started as

A 1931 *Stamford* shape *Early Morning set* in *Apples.*

A *Stamford* shape *Early Morning set* in the 1931 *Tennis* design, this example showing that sometimes these sets were sold with two plates.

a paintress and Clarice chose her to supervise the shop. The *Bizarre* girls were now confident young women and enjoyed short motorbike jaunts with their boyfriends in the hills around Staffordshire, or playing tennis at Wolstanton. Clarice's social life, however, continued to revolve around the factory and Colley. She had little time to relax, but rewarded herself for her hard work by replacing her old car with a brand-new Austin Pearl Seven Cabriolet. Any woman driving herself around Stoke-on-Trent raised more than a few eyebrows, but, stylish in every respect, Clarice paid extra to have it coach-painted in grey with ruby red seats. It did not reflect a glamorous lifestyle, since it was often still parked at the factory as she worked late, long after her girls had left to go out for the evening.

Clarice's thirty-seventh birthday was on 20 January 1936, the day King George V died. This and the abdication crisis that ensued set the tone for change in Britain. Newport Pottery and Wilkinson's rationalized their production methods and ranges, and although some *Bizarre* and *Fantasque* designs continued to be produced, from the middle of that year ware was marked just *Clarice Cliff*. Production of the Art Deco *Stamford* and *Conical* teaware shapes ceased. Only the *Bon Jour* was to survive to the end of the decade. The trend was for functional tableware, and the public seemed to lose interest in frivolous teapots. The royal abdication in December echoed the end of the *Bizarre* era, and although Clarice did not know it at the time, a few years later her life was to change as dramatically as that of the King and Wallis Simpson.

In response to the shrinking home market a major export drive was mounted. The effort put into selling Clarice's pottery abroad was shown by a display staged in Australia at Scott's Hotel in Melbourne. Thirty tables, and wall displays, were piled high with dinnerware, tea- and coffee sets, lamp bases and fancies. Colley Shorter's overseas dealers distributed Clarice's pottery to many corners of the globe. This wide availability helped establish its collectability when *Bizarre* was later rediscovered by Art Deco enthusiasts in the Seventies.

The girls' hand-painting demonstrations around Britain continued. A display of a vivid new landscape called *Forest Glen* formed the backdrop to paintresses Nancy Dale and Lily Barrow at James Colmer's store in Bath. At Welwyn Garden City paintress Rene Dale spoke to a man who was clearly captivated by her hand-painting. She only discovered as he left that she had just met the sculptor Henry Moore.

Most of the new teaware shapes produced between 1936 and 1939 featured natural finishes. The heavily textured *Corncob* and *Raffia* contrasted with the more sophisticated teapot, milk and sugar based on a shell shape, called *Nautilus*. A large teapot modelled as a *Rooster* was also marketed, but the most popular of Clarice's later shapes was the conservative *Windsor* teaware.

A *Tee Pee* teapot, which had a totem-pole handle and an Indian-chief spout, was designed before the war but not put into production. It was the work of apprentice modeller Betty Silvester under Clarice's supervision. Finally made for export in the Fifties, it had a 'Greetings from Canada' backstamp. Ironically, many examples returned to Britain as presents.

The factory wound down production as orders diminished, so Clarice had more time to devote to her first love of modelling. Amazingly, along with her work for Newport Pottery, Clarice had also since the late Twenties acted as a modeller for the Shorter & Sons factory in Stoke (jointly managed by Colley and his brother Guy). Some of Clarice's Newport Pottery ware from the late Thirties is more in the style she used for Shorter's. A hippopotamus ashtray with an open mouth to hold the cigarette, and a dove ashtray with an aperture between the bird's tail feathers, are typical and show that she never lost her sense of humour.

The impact of war on Newport and Wilkinson's was immediate. Functional decorated ware was sold in bulk to the War Office, and during the first year most of Clarice's paintresses left to serve the war effort in munitions factories or in the Forces. The most significant event in 1939 for Clarice and Colley, however, was the death of Colley's wife in November after a long illness. Mindful of attracting gossip, they wed secretly in December 1940. Only a few friends and family knew. It was not until a year later that they let it be known generally, and in wartime such news was unimportant.

Clarice Cliff-Shorter's life took on a new colour. Colley's world was now hers. Chetwynd House, nestling in the hills at Clayton to the west of Stoke, dated from 1899, when it had been designed and built by Parker & Unwin. It was filled with fine art, Georgian silver and Japanese sword fittings, which were Colley's pride and joy. In the garages were two Rolls-Royce cars, but because of wartime petrol rationing the couple often travelled into Stoke in a horse and buggy.

Clarice became hostess to Colley's friends and business acquaintances, but with two servants and little to do she was drawn more and more to the magnificent grounds around Chetwynd House. She had never had a garden before, and now suddenly she had one of five acres! It cascaded gently down the hillside and had wonderful views across the valley. Clumps of mature hydrangeas and rhododendrons were interspersed with archways of old-fashioned 'Danse de Feu' roses. One area had a disused Twenties tennis court covered with lupins that had self-seeded. Rocky borders were smothered in rich blue gentians and high holly hedges were full of wild birds. Clarice had inherited a real *My Garden*, which she shared with Colley.

Within a year of the war ending Clarice and Colley threw themselves back into their factories. Clarice re-established a small hand-painting shop, this time at Wilkinson's, and various 'girls', who were now nearly forty, returned to work. But tastes had changed and hand-painting was really an indulgence in a factory

A *Bon Jour* shape teapot from 1934 in *Crocus*.

Clarice and Colley on holiday in Acapulco in the Fifties.

A *Bon Jour* shape teapot in *Nasturtium*, and *Strawberry set* in *Nasturtium*, both from 1932.

where most of the output was of printed ware. Regulations did not allow decorated ware except for export, and the overseas market was highly traditional between 1946 and 1952. Eventually production of decorated ware was permitted again for home consumption, but there was no opportunity for Clarice to design new teaware. Tea was rationed until 1952, so people needed fewer teapots.

Having modernized his factories after the war, Colley gradually delegated his work at Wilkinson's to Norman Smith, who had joined in 1940. Colley's daughter Joan had married a Canadian service man, so he spent much time on 'business trips' to Canada. Clarice accompanied him on some visits, while on other occasions she would stay at Chetwynd entertaining her sisters and their children in her garden. Less involved now in the creative side of the factory, in 1951 she appointed a young Art Director named Eric Elliot.

In 1952 Colley was seventy years old, and when Clarice suffered ill-health in October it spurred them on to spend more time together. They went on further business trips around the world, which were thinly disguised holidays. In between they enjoyed the house and garden of Chetwynd, or took chauffeur-driven trips to Devon, Dorset or Kent. They relished their years together before Colley's death in 1963, aged eighty-one.

Clarice sold the factories to Midwinter Pottery and retreated to Chetwynd House. Apart from visits from her family, she now led a very quiet life. One of her helpers

A picture taken by Clarice of Colley Shorter relaxing in the garden of Chetwynd House in September 1957, when he was seventy-five years old.

Clarice enjoying some early evening gardening at Chetwynd in a picture taken by Colley in 1957.

was Reg Lamb, whom she had first met in 1919 when he had purloined modelling clays for her. Her time was fully occupied with cleaning the antiques in the house and tending the garden. She avoided contact with a growing band of *Bizarre* ware collectors, although eventually she begrudgingly assisted the organizers of the first exhibition of her work. She wrote about this in 1972 to her former assistant Hilda Lovatt, who had become a lifelong friend.

I shall have to write a separate letter about an exhibition of Clarice Cliff in Brighton which has caused me weeks of work! I have been trying to get out of it for weeks and months but Mr Guy gave them my address when he saw an advertisement in The Times, *and they finally got my telephone number and bothered the life out of me.*

Clarice never went to the exhibition but she donated some pieces of *Bizarre* to Brighton Museum and wrote brief notes for the catalogue. She died suddenly on 23 October 1972. Fittingly, in the same – her last – letter to Hilda she nostalgically recalled Crocus, the flower that had been associated with her since 1928.

Every time I look out and see the Jasmine I think of you, it is so cheerful. The pink heather Queen Mary, and King George the red, is a lovely show, I must get some nearer the house. The Snowdrops are through but I think that they are later than usual. There is a patch of orange Crocus under the window where it is warmer, but all the rest are only shewing [sic] the green tips yet. It is lovely to think that Spring is not far away.

Paintress Rene Dale remembers Clarice Cliff

'Clarice Cliff was a quietly spoken woman, whom I had known since childhood. Her niece Nancy, as well as being my cousin, was a good friend. Her mother, Clarice's sister Sarah, brought Nancy up at the family house in Tunstall after the death of her husband in the First World War. I used to join them for Sunday tea at their home during the Twenties. I remember one time when we had stew, Clarice shook the pepper-pot over her plate so vigorously that the top came off. We all fell about laughing!

'After seeing my paintings from school, Clarice promised that if I attended art school she would find me a position with the newly formed *Bizarre* "girls". I joined the *Bizarre* shop in 1931 and, after nearly a year of painting "strokes" of all shapes, which had to be rubbed off time and time again until perfect, I was allowed to paint the bees on the lids of the *Beehive* honey pots. The actual pots were painted by the older girls, but it was a start.

'One highlight I remember was the installation of a wireless so that we could listen to plays and songs while we worked. This was quite unheard-of in those days, and kept us quiet and busy at the same time.

'"Miss Cliff", as we had to call her, was very strict and wouldn't let any work pass that was not to her liking. On the other hand, she could be very friendly and a joke never went amiss. She arranged Christmas parties and outings to Staffordshire beauty-spots and the seaside. Twice we were roped in for charity fêtes, appearing on floats in various forms of fancy dress. One float was based around the *Bizooka*, a mock-up of a horse made of plates, vases and candlesticks and anything else that would fit. This was Clarice's brainwave. Each fête ended with a dance at the Town Hall.

'Periodically some girls were chosen to demonstrate *Bizarre* hand-painting in the crockery department of stores up and down the country. These demonstrations usually lasted three weeks, and we thought it was wonderful to be chosen. On one occasion a small boy asked to paint a plate. As it was quite good I told him to sign it, and said I would have it fired and sent to him if "Miss Cliff" agreed, which she did. One year when we went to Hastings, the materials we used and the potter's wheel to demonstrate how banding was done had been sent ahead by rail, but failed to arrive. We spent the whole time on the beach. What an unexpected holiday!

'The war came as a hiccup in the *Bizarre* years. Some of us went to munitions and others to the Forces, and decorated ware became minimal. After the war it was never the same, with different people working in a different building. The old *Bizarre* shop had done its share of war-work, as it had been used as a store for the army,

Bizarre 'girl' Rene Dale pictured with Leonard Griffin in 1990.

and we never went back to it. A lot of old girls returned, and Clarice was now designing new patterns and shapes, but dear old *Crocus* never died. Neither did any of Clarice Cliff's original teapots!'

(Rene Dale was a Clarice Cliff paintress from 1931 to 1952, except for the war years. Later she worked for Studio Szeiler Pottery in Stoke. Although she retired in 1979, Rene now attends evening classes in watercolour painting in Burslem, where she still lives. Every year she attends a reunion of the *Bizarre* girls.)

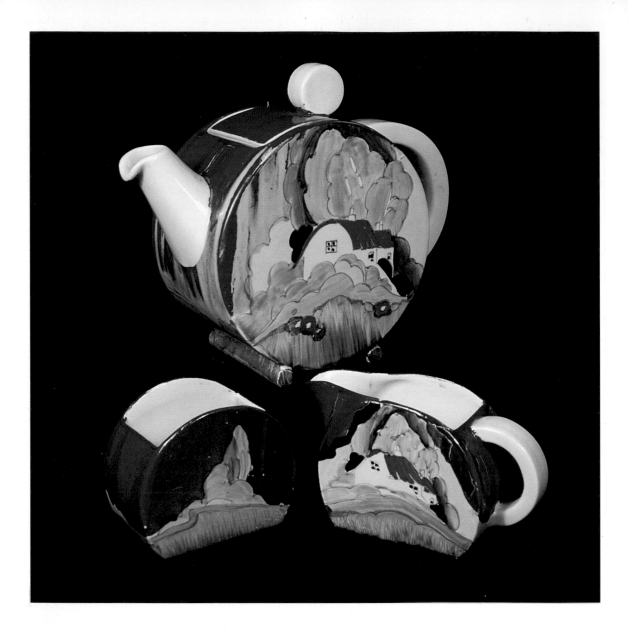

Clarice's tremendous teapots

Tea enthusiasts have for centuries enjoyed the ritual of preparing, serving and drinking teas in many forms. The evolution of the teaset was closely linked to the gradual changes in how tea was served. It seems hard to believe now that early teacups did not have what we regard as the essential handle. Amazingly, the Chinese, creators of the teapot, only used it to hold boiling water. The tea leaves were already in the cup – and they just poured the water on to them.

Chinese tea was available in Britain from around 1650, but was a luxury. Such was its expense that tea was put into containers known as 'tea caddies', which were kept under strict lock and key by the mistress of the house. The tea caddy, or 'kati', originated in China and the name referred to a measurement of weight. As tea did not become part of our social culture immediately, few people owned a teapot.

A *Bon Jour* shape tea trio in *Forest Glen* from 1935 to 1936.

When Catherine of Braganza came to Britain from Portugal to marry Charles II she had already acquired a taste for tea drinking, and so popularized it both at Court and further afield in the 1660s. Interest in tea grew partly because of its exotic origins; some people believed it had medicinal qualities and so it was also sold in apothecary shops. However, a tea tax was imposed, resulting in a black market. Tea gardens evolved in the late seventeenth century in response to women being banned from coffee houses. Eventually the tea-shop became a place where women could meet and take tea together.

The milk jug was possibly a later addition, as tea was drunk 'black' for the first hundred years. When delicate teacups were introduced in the middle of the eighteenth century, milk was added first to reduce the risk of them cracking from the boiling water.

In 1784 tea duties were abolished and tea drinking became more widespread. From the 1830s, when the Opium Wars cut off China as a supplier, tea was grown in India. The tea plant flourished in India and later it was found that it had actually originated there. Within a few years tea became the drink of the masses in Britain.

In the Victorian era 'teatime' became a meal, and it was at this stage that plates were added to the tea service. Every home had a teapot, and the vast majority of these were manufactured in Staffordshire. By the Thirties, therefore, Britain had been a tea-drinking nation for only one hundred years, even though tea had arrived nearly three centuries earlier. The most popular brew in Britain's Art Deco cups was of tea from India or Ceylon, often branded as 'Empire Tea'.

Closely linked to Britain's love of tea is an affection for teaware, and in particular the teapot. Essentially a functional item, teapots are rarely treated as such. Buying a new teapot was (and is) more dictated by style than necessity. Many homes have too many teapots, although perhaps the owners might argue that it is not possible to have too many!

Had Clarice Cliff not acquired the habit of drinking tea from her parents, she would certainly have been converted by Colley Shorter. Their almost daily meetings in her studio, held over copious cups of tea, were noticed by many Newport Pottery workers. When she rose to become Art Director of the factory, Clarice also became one of the first women actually to design a teapot.

Clarice's factory made formal teasets, which had six cups and saucers, six tea plates, a cake plate, a milk jug, sugar bowl and a large teapot. However, life changed in the Twenties and Thirties when the *Early Morning set* was the most popular form of teaset. It comprised a teapot, two cups and saucers, a milk and sugar, and one or possibly two plates. Sometimes these sets were even sold with a matching ceramic tray.

The term *Early Morning set* referred to the tradition of a couple having tea in bed, at the start of a day. Either the man or the woman would get up, make the tea, and serve it on a tray. Most sets were sold with just one plate, which it seems was used for a simple slice of buttered toast, cut into halves, which the couple shared. This morning ritual was a Thirties echo of the days when the landed gentry had tea served in bed by their servants. *Early Morning set* was a term that manufacturers used at the time, but Thirties devotees and many Clarice Cliff collectors now call them *tea for two* sets. This name does not seem to have caught on quickly, for the song 'Tea for Two' had débuted in 1925 in the musical *No, No Nanette*. Edward Bramah of the Bramah Tea and Coffee Museum commented:

The origin of the name for trade purposes is interesting since it reminds us of something often overlooked nowadays, that 'tea for two' was made when somebody called round for tea. The phrase naturally extended into the tea shops which were so popular when Clarice Cliff was active in the market. Sometimes a better expression is created than the one originally used at the factory. The term tea for two *has more of a ring to it than* Early Morning set.

We do not know if Clarice's parents maintained the tradition of having early morning tea together, but it seems likely that they did. With seven children the small kitchen would have been full in the morning, so they probably had their first 'cuppa' in the bedroom, before going downstairs to join in the hubbub of family life.

When Clarice left school her first job was at Lingard Webster in Tunstall, and we know that she gilded many of their traditional teapots. The Potteries had been Britain's main manufacturer of teaware for centuries, yet the actual shape of everyday teapots had barely changed.

Clarice loved modelling, and just before her own name appeared on ware she was asked by Colley Shorter to design and produce a range of children's teaware. The

67

imaginative results included her *Bones the Butcher* teapot. Colley cleverly marketed it as being designed by 'Joan Shorter Aged 8'. Linking the ware to his younger daughter inspired publicity, featuring Joan talking about her teaware for children. Shorter's promotional flair is impressive when one notes that this was four years before Shirley Temple's film début in *Red Haired Alibi*. Most importantly, the use of a real person to promote ceramics may have been the catalyst for the appearance of Clarice's name on ware a few months later.

When she started designing for Newport Pottery Clarice inherited some very old-fashioned teapot shapes. One of these, the *Globe,* was typical of the traditional Stoke-on-Trent shape, which can be traced back at least as far as 1750. And the *Athens* teapot, with its faceted sides, was based on the style of metal teapots popular in the previous century. Although not ideally suited to Clarice's original *Bizarre* designs, these shapes continued to be used as part of her range until the mid- to late Thirties.

By August 1929 the innovative vases and bowls that Clarice had produced in her *Conical* series were selling well, and she decided to add a teaware shape to the range. For the body of the shape she took the simple form of a cone, and for the handle the shape of the triangular feet of her *Conical* bowls – but, most unusually, the handle was solid. The spout was also extraordinary in that each side was straight – it was basically a pyramid hanging on the side of the pot. Although the *Conical* teapot was eventually produced in three sizes, the first issued was the two-cup size, specifically for an *Early Morning set*, so the importance of these sets at the time is clear.

Clarice modelled *Conical* cups that had completely straight sides, unlike the factory's traditional shapes, and the triangular handle on these was also solid. The design of the sugar bowl was obvious – it was just a miniature version of the *Conical* bowl she had already designed with four triangular feet. The milk was even more novel, being a very steep cone on four bladed feet. Indeed, in sticking to the style of the design and ignoring its function, Clarice produced a rather impractical shape, as it held very little milk. This was the first part of the *Conical Early Morning set* to be adapted; a larger, re-styled version appeared within a year. Teasets with the original milk jug are now comparatively rare.

The *Conical Early Morning set* was an instant success. It was not functional but it *was* fun. The solid handle on the teapot was liable to get too hot to hold, when the pot was full of boiling tea. This did not deter would-be buyers but ensured a healthy flow of orders for matchings at the factory, to replace dropped pieces!

Looking at the contemporary products of Clarice's competitors, one appreciates how ahead of their time her new ceramic shapes were in Britain. None of the other Stoke-on-Trent factories had a *moderne* shape, as it was then called. For a year the *Conical* had no competition, but inevitably copies appeared. The first was by Shelley

Potteries, a manufacturer of high-quality bone china. Its designer Eric Slater produced what was basically Clarice's *Conical* teapot shape with a foot added. Being in bone china it was sold in delicate designs, and although the shape was similar it looked more sophisticated, but less exciting. Slater's cups also had solid triangular handles, but these were almost immediately changed to open ones, whereas Clarice persisted with the impractical but stylish solid ones until as late as 1936.

During 1930 Clarice issued four- and six-cup sizes of the *Conical* teapot. With solid handles these would have been impossible to hold when full of tea, so the handles were made 'open'. However, these larger sets, generally sold with four or six cups, saucers and plates, did not sell as well as the *Early Morning sets* and are now harder to find.

Almost before Shelley Potteries had time to issue its copy of her *Conical* shape, Clarice produced another new teapot, which she called the *Stamford*. Issued in September 1930, it was equally innovative. Constructed from a mixture of curved and straight lines, it was basically D-shaped, and its most notable quality was its two *flat* sides.

Clarice did not actually design the *Stamford* herself. She discovered the shape in *Mobilier et Décoration*, a French design magazine. The original, by the French silversmiths Tétard Frères, was a luxury item made for a wealthy French actor. The teapot, milk and sugar were basically circular, with one or two straight edges. Clarice gave her modellers and casters the challenge of constructing

An advertising photograph taken by Clarice Cliff in 1931 showing a *Stamford* shape teapot in *Tennis*, and a *Stamford* tea caddy in *Autumn*.

suitable moulds to produce them. The *Stamford* milk jugs and sugar bowls needed special supports in the bottle-oven when they were fired, to stop the flat sides warping. Clarice did not design geometrically shaped cups for the set, but used those from the *Conical* set.

The *Stamford* teapot is a very special piece. When it first appeared it was both technically and aesthetically innovative; no ceramic designer before Clarice Cliff had ever tried to make such a geometric form. The earthenware manufacturing process was adept at making round, flowing shapes, but it took time and ingenuity to construct the moulds for the *Stamford*. Its square corners, oblong section spout and geometrically shaped surfaces have an architectural quality that pre-dates the style of Odeon cinema interiors and exteriors.

The decoration of the *Stamford* teapot is one of its most appealing features. The flat front and back served as a 'canvas' for many of Clarice's designs. Although the revolutionary *Conical* shape was suited to her *Bizarre* and *Fantasque* patterns, the *Stamford*'s flat sides showed them off to even better advantage. The combination of form and design was not harmonious, but that was never Clarice's intention. *Bizarre* was meant to startle and surprise, and even amuse. Certainly it shocked many of the older buyers in the early Thirties, but it was this visual impact that created the vogue for her teasets.

The *Stamford Early Morning set* was immediately successful, to the extent that even Tétard Frères in Paris became aware of it. Clarice and Colley were eventually

Stamford shape teaware in
Pastel Melon from 1932.

A *Bon Jour* shape *Early Morning* set in *Rudyard* from 1933 to 1934.

visited by Jean Tétard and amicably paid him for the rights to reproduce his shape, which by that time was making the factory a large profit.

Colley Shorter was a teapot connoisseur. He encouraged Clarice to develop more shapes, and played an active role in adapting her designs to ensure that as well as being modern the teapot was functional. The *Stamford* teapot was originally issued with a square-lipped spout, which was stylistically perfect for its geometric form. Colley was critical of its pouring, however, so Clarice had to adapt it, and a new version with a drooping spout appeared.

Later in 1930 Clarice designed another new teapot shape. Delightful in its simplicity, the *Eton* consisted of a tubular body with angular handle and spout, topped by a square, mortar-board-style lid. Clarice did not design a matching milk and sugar, but a coffee-pot and large water jug were added to the range. *Eton* was not a big seller despite its unusual shape. It was produced in limited quantities until 1936.

Clarice never made a *Stamford* shape coffee-pot, but in the following year somebody else did! Lawleys, which was a major customer for *Bizarre*, instigated the production of a coffee-pot and teapot, obviously copied from the *Stamford*. To change the lines, the front was angular rather than curved, and it was given a triangular handle obviously inspired by Clarice's *Conical* ware; otherwise it was identical. The glaze was a thicker, more custard-coloured version of the honeyglaze used on

Bizarre, and it was issued in a freehand geometric design.

The only new aspect of the Lawleys pieces was the name of the 'designer' on the base. Surprisingly, it was that of the actress and film star Edna Best, whom they paid to endorse the ware. She was a well-established name in Britain, having starred with Noël Coward in the play *The Constant Nymph* in 1926. Clarice and Colley must have been very flattered, if not a little annoyed, about this imitation of both the design and innovative promotional methods they had pioneered with *Bizarre.* We know that after this Colley Shorter registered Clarice's major new shapes, which is why a registered number is found on the base of many teapots. It was ironic, though, that Jean Tétard was copied by Clarice, and Clarice was then imitated by Edna Best.

Yet another new teaware range was called *Daffodil.* This appeared as a full set with its own milk and sugar, and even cups with daffodil-shaped handles. The body was based on the shape of the flower and the solid handles were gently corrugated, making them a little more practical than those on the *Conical* cups. The *Daffodil* range, with its softer curvilinear shapes more reminiscent of Art Nouveau, was another runaway success for Clarice. In London at the First Avenue Hotel personalities hired to endorse *Bizarre* included actresses Marie Tempest and Adrienne Allen, and entertainer Leslie Henson. Shorter was not reticent about having his picture taken with them – and naturally they were drinking out of *Daffodil*-shape ware!

Colley Shorter (left) taking tea – from Clarice's *Daffodil* shape cups – with the actresses Marie Tempest and Adrienne Allen and the entertainer Leslie Henson at a London promotion in 1932.

An original advertising picture taken by Clarice Cliff of an *Eton* shape teapot with a *Stamford* sugar, and *Conical* cups and saucers in the 1933 *Secrets* design.

A *Trieste* shape *Early Morning set* complete with a matching pottery tray in the 1934 *Rhodanthe* pattern.

The influence of Art Deco had waned in continental Europe by 1933, but in Britain it was growing. The Hoover Factory, a definitive Art Deco building designed by Wallis Gilbert & Partners, had become an architectural landmark by 1932. In 1933 plans were drawn up by Eric Mendelsohn and Serge Chermayeff for the De La Warr pavilion at Bexhill-on-Sea, which was completed by 1936. This architectural style was as much inspired by Hollywood's version of Art Deco as by the European one.

Clarice seemed to be more in tune with the ideas she absorbed from the Continent, and some of her fancies around this time can be traced to originals by the Austrian designer and architect Josef Hoffmann. Once again, however, Paris was the inspiration for her newest teaware shape, as its name *Bon Jour* indicated. It was a clever development of the *Stamford* shape: Clarice simply turned the D shape into an O. The round, flat-sided body of the teapot was supported on small tubular feet, again inspired by a Tétard Frères original. The sugar was taken from the *Stamford* set, but the milk was custom-designed.

By the time *Bon Jour* ware was issued, Clarice had changed her palette to more subtle colours. The early geometric and abstract designs gave way to vibrant floral ones, such as *Gardenia* and *Nasturtium*, and various landscapes including *May Avenue*. Clarice had not lost her sense of fun, however, and just by adding a clock face to the teapot of the *Bon Jour* set she created her simple but stunning *Eight o'clock* ware.

Since the launch of *Bizarre*, Clarice's tableware had

always sold well – particularly her dinner sets with their futuristic tureens, the *Stamford* and *Odilon*, both of which were unmistakably shaped like flying saucers. In 1933 a major addition to her tableware range was the exotically named *Biarritz*. Here she took elements from various shapes and incorporated them into what was to become her most stylish ware. The plates were square or oblong with a circular central well, and the tureens semi-circular and flat-sided with oblong lids. The range immediately sold well, although it was ahead of its time, both stylistically and technically, and the factory again had numerous problems firing the square plates and flat-sided tureens. It even offered a unique personalized service of incorporating the customer's initials as a motif in platinum on the ware.

Despite the extra cost entailed in manufacturing, *Biarritz* ware was extremely popular. When demand started to outstrip supply, dealers in North America even ordered it undecorated, as the shape was so novel. To match her *Bon Jour* teasets to the *Biarritz* shape Clarice issued them with oblong saucers. These sets were one of the last flowerings of the true Art Deco style made at the factory.

In 1933 the owner of Werner Brothers Store of East London, South Africa, a family business that included a selection of exclusive ceramics, went on a European buying trip with his family. In England they visited Newport Pottery to order goods, and met Clarice. She was enchanted with their three-year-old daughter Sheila

Sheila Murray aged three at Newport Pottery in 1933, with Clarice Cliff (right) and her mother.

A *Daffodil* shape teapot in *Honolulu* from 1934.

The complete six-person
child's teaset in *Honolulu*
produced by Clarice for Sheila
Murray.

and had the idea of creating a special *Bizarre* six-person child's teaset for her. She knew of some small cups, saucers and plates in a warehouse at the factory, left over from the Twenties when miniature teasets for children had been popular. Clarice combined these old shapes with the smallest *Globe* teapot, milk and sugar. Each piece was then carefully decorated in miniature in the new *Honolulu* pattern. Shortly after Sheila returned to South Africa the package arrived. Along with the teaset Clarice had included photographs of Sheila and her together, with a card that said: 'To Sheila with kindest regards from Clarice Cliff. Some day perhaps I may have a cup of tea with you . . .'

Two teaware shapes appeared around this time that were dramatically different from the *Biarritz* ware. *Trieste* was a geometrically based set, whereas *Lynton* with its ribbed body simulated a hand-thrown look. Every piece of the teaware for both sets matched, and as the factory sold more of the *Lynton*, this may have given Clarice and Colley a clear indication of changing tastes. After 1935 Clarice's teapots bore little resemblance to her earlier Jazz Age ones. Her inspiration now came from more natural forms. There were to be no more geometric shapes.

Clarice was amazingly productive between 1936 and 1939, but her more visually conservative teapots relied on surface texture with little colour, the trend being for more muted ware. Typical of this period were her *Corncob*, *Nautilus* and *Raffia* shapes. While these were ingenious, the teaware produced as part of the *Celtic*

The card Clarice sent to Sheila with the teaset.

The rare *Bizarre* envelope in which the card was sent.

Harvest range in 1938 was by comparison ordinary, with embossed flowers, fruit and wheat sheaves totally covering the body. Interestingly, apart from the *Bon Jour* teapot, which was produced until 1940, her best-selling shape at this time was the *Windsor*. This very orthodox teapot, with its regal name, was extremely appropriate for the new mood of the country.

As the prospect of war became a reality, people wrapped their *Early Morning sets* in newspaper and stored them in attics or cupboards. The Jazz Age that had fuelled Art Deco faded to a memory. Like Clarice's *Bizarre* teapots, it lay awaiting rediscovery in the Seventies.

A stylish 1937 advertisement for *Clarice Cliff* ware after the *Bizarre* trademark had been dropped, featuring a *Bon Jour* teapot in the *Hollyhocks* design.

The instant teapot guide

Between 1928 and 1939 Clarice Cliff designed more than twenty teapots. She also produced about ten coffee-pot shapes, and for children a *Chick Cocoa pot* and the *Bones the Butcher* teapot. For many of these shapes she made complementary milk jugs, sugar bowls, cups and saucers. Together with a vast number of unusual vases, bowls and fancies, she achieved the unprecedented total of more than 700 shapes in ten years.

Her teapots were produced in various sizes. The factory classified these as 42s, 36s, 30s and 24s. The logical conclusion that the highest number is for the biggest teapot is paradoxically *not* the case. Confusingly for collectors, these numbers actually refer to the quantity of teapots of a particular size that would fit into a standard saggar for firing – so twenty-four of the larger teapots would fill the same size saggar as forty-two of the smallest. The largest teapot for a six-person teaset was a 24, while for an *Early Morning set* a 42 teapot was used. You will find most Clarice Cliff teapot shapes in at least two of these sizes.

The success of a teaset pivots on the overall design of the teapot. Not only does it need to be functional, it should also be adaptable to other pieces in the set. The *Conical* teaset was in this sense artistically good, but with both the milk and sugar being extremely small, function was obviously sacrificed to design. The aesthetic advantage is that often the sugar bowl has the whole pattern in miniature. It is found both radially or as an overall pattern, and it is hard to imagine how the decorators painted it.

The cup from the *Conical* teaset, with its solid triangular handle and cleanly formed body, fits well with other shapes, and Clarice was to utilize it for many of her later teaware sets.

Although they were probably made in larger quantities than the *Stamford*, many *Conical* sets now lack the teapot, because the solid triangular handle transmitted heat from the pot and they were frequently dropped. The four- and six-cup sizes always had open handles for this reason.

Clarice's *Stamford* shape teaware was as stylish as the *Conical* but more functional. As well as providing a perfect surface for decoration, the flat-sided teapot, milk and sugar fitted easily on to a tray. Indeed, such was its popularity that a special tray was made and sold with later sets. Clarice did not design original teacup shapes for this set but used her *Conical* ones, which suited it well. The milk and sugar were a more practical size and, most importantly, with an easy-to-hold handle the teapot was more likely to remain intact. In a recent survey of collectors of Clarice Cliff, the *Stamford* was voted their favourite of all her teapots.

By the time Clarice's third major teaware shape – *Bon Jour* – was issued the factory was more adept at manufacturing her demanding shapes. The round body

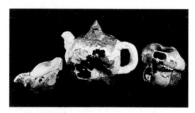

One of Clarice's failures, the unpredictably shaped *Le Bon Dieu* ware from 1932.

The *Nautilus* shape teapot was made as a trial in 1935 but seems never to have been put into production.

'Gay Gifts', a rare example of Clarice Cliff colour advertising in a feature from Christmas 1933, shows a *Bon Jour* shape *Early Morning set* in Clarice's inventive *Eight o'clock* design.

A rare *Bon Jour* shape *Early
Morning set* in *May Avenue* from
1933.

achieved a more delicate effect than the D-shaped *Stamford*, yet being flat-sided it had the same functional advantages. Clarice had absorbed the work of many other designers, and she embellished the shape of the *Bon Jour* teapot with a very Art Deco pastille-shaped knob on the lid. This small detail, copied from some tea- and coffeeware she had seen several years earlier designed by Margarete Heymann-Loëbenstein, was exactly right. The *Stamford* sugar bowl fitted perfectly, but a new milk jug was produced with a *Bon Jour* shape handle. Otherwise the cups and saucers used initially were those from the *Conical* set.

When *Biarritz* tableware was introduced to complement the *Bon Jour* tea- and coffeeware, some sets were issued with oblong saucers. This means that an *Early Morning set* can include a mixture of a *Bon Jour* teapot with *Conical* shape cups on *Biarritz* saucers, and a *Stamford* sugar! This is a nightmare for both collectors and writers on Clarice Cliff. A few collectors have been lucky enough to discover actual *Bon Jour* cups, which have a handle similar in shape to that on the teapot. These are generally teamed with the oblong saucers but were produced in limited quantities.

After *Conical, Stamford* and *Bon Jour,* Clarice's most collectable teapots are her *Eton, Daffodil* and *Trieste* shapes. However, evidence from collections suggests that these were also produced in limited quantities. This rarity was probably dictated by the commercial pressures on Clarice as she concentrated on her most commercial

The heavily modelled 1937 to 1938 *Raffia* ware, including a teapot and milk jug, seen here with some dishes and a flower jug.

An *Early Morning set* in Clarice's 1938 *Corncob* range.

wares to attract sales during the Depression. The *Eton* is possibly the most innovative of the three. The decorators occasionally had the opportunity to paint part of the design on its square lid and these pieces are extremely desirable.

The graceful *Daffodil* shape was first issued in a pale pink all-over glaze called *Damask Rose*, featuring only small freehand motifs. Later it was issued in assorted *Bizarre* and *Fantasque* designs. The *Honolulu* example pictured in this book is a truly *Bizarre* combination of design and shape and, unfortunately for today's collectors, a rarity. The *Daffodil* teaset cups have open handles, but you may also find the slightly smaller coffee cups with a solid handle.

Trieste appeared after these other innovative teapots in 1934, and is mainly found in simpler tableware designs, but a few examples in *Coral Firs* or *Forest Glen* are known.

Clarice's traditional *Lynton* shape ware actually pre-dates the more stylish *Trieste,* so it is found in a larger range of designs. All the pieces including the plate and cups were designed for the range, and the complete *Early Morning set* in this shape in *Coral Firs* shows how different the effect was of imposing a landscape on a textured shape.

Modelled teapot shapes range from the simple early *Marguerite* ware, through the disastrous *Le Bon Dieu* to the over-fussy *Celtic Harvest* ware of the late Thirties. Probably the most successful of Clarice's heavily modelled teaware shapes were the *Corncob* and *Raffia*, which are also proving to be collectable.

A *Stamford* tea and hot water set on a matching tray in a simple banded design from 1933 to 1935.

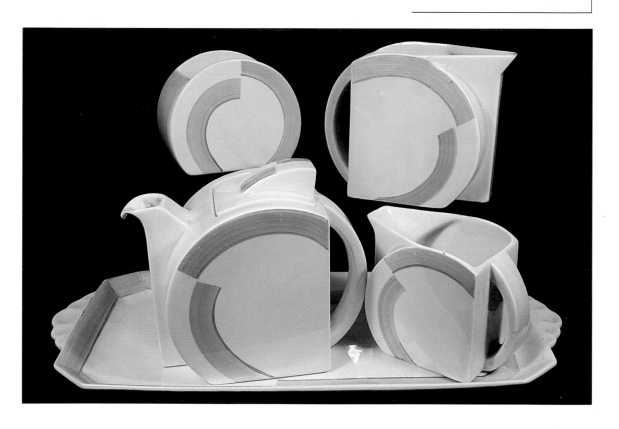

When looking at an *Early Morning set* or a four- or six-person teaset, it is wise to check the shapes of the milk and sugar. Sometimes when stock was low in the glost warehouse the *Bon Jour* milk jug was substituted for the very similar *Stamford*. Collectors will also find it confusing that the cups with solid triangular handles, designed for the *Conical* teaware, were also used for *all* the *Stamford* sets, and even the majority of the *Bon Jour* sets. The vast range of Clarice's teaware shapes meant that it simply was not possible to make individually shaped items for each set.

Clarice's strength was that not only did she function as a designer of shapes for Newport Pottery, she also devised the patterns to go on them. Teapots were decorated in patterns from various ranges, including *Bizarre*, *Fantasque*, *Inspiration*, *Latona*, *Appliqué*, *Delecia* and *Moderne*. Literally hundreds of different patterns will be found, but generally, almost regardless of pattern, collectors will find that the more colour a piece has, the more expensive it will be. Later teaware, such as *Honeydew*, with just a small floral motif will be more affordable and is a good way to start a collection of Clarice Cliff teapots.

Clarice Cliff ware is marked with a backstamp, which is nearly always the name of a range, not of a particular design. Where it includes the words *Bizarre by Clarice Cliff* it almost certainly dates from between 1928 and 1936. Later ware just has her name, with either Newport Pottery or Wilkinson's credited. The markings are

The classic *Bizarre* backstamp.

numerous and often raise more questions than they answer. Sometimes a hand-painted pattern name will be seen above a backstamp: *Crocus* often appears in green above a *Bizarre* mark. In addition to her mass of teaware, Clarice's huge range of shapes meant that even the workers in charge of the pattern and order books were sometimes confused. Pieces were given the wrong backstamp or even left the factory unmarked. Teasets were a particular problem. The 'missus' would assemble the different shapes needed to complete a set and take them into the shop for decorating, so that even the marks on an original set may vary. A categorization of backstamps is included in the book *Clarice Cliff – the Bizarre Affair.*

New collectors are inevitably attracted to Clarice's teapots. It *is* possible to find single teapots, as they were listed individually on the original factory price-sheets, but the majority were sold as part of a set. Alternatively, for the devotee whose budget does not yet stretch to a full *Early Morning set,* a good way to begin a collection is to buy individual cups and saucers. With so much variety in both shape and pattern, these could prove extremely addictive, as it would be impossible to assemble every combination!

Tea drinking accessories that you may find include the *Stamford* shape tea caddy. Confusingly, this was also sold as both a biscuit jar and (minus the lid) as a vase to display flowers. Another collecting theme would be to look out for unusual items of teaware, such as strawberry

A *Stamford* teapot in *Orange Roof Cottage* from 1932 to 1934.

sets, a tray with a fitted sugar and cream, used outdoors in the Thirties on lazy summer days. The preference for a covered sugar in Europe, and other parts of the world where *Bizarre* was sold, meant that the shapes used for sets varied depending on the country of destination. You may be lucky enough to find a rarity such as the *Conical* covered sugar in *Honolulu,* which we discovered when taking photographs for this book.

A few pieces are found with custom E P N S stands or fittings. Originally sold from jewellers, these may comprise a milk and sugar on a fitment, or several *Biarritz* plates stacked to form a cake-stand to be used for afternoon tea.

There was negative inflation for part of the Thirties, so it is hard to compare prices for teapots and teasets over the whole period. However, as a comparison, the *Bizarre* girls were paid about six to seven shillings each for a five-and-a-half-day week in 1929, whereas by 1935 they were earning between thirty shillings and two pounds. For interest we have included on pp.104–111 original prices for some of the shapes listed. Typically, a single *Stamford* teapot cost between six and nine shillings in 1931, and a full *Early Morning set* in the *Stamford, Conical* or *Bon Jour* shapes between eleven and eighteen shillings. The price depended on the pattern on the set.

If you start a collection of Clarice Cliff teaware, remember a few simple tricks. When evaluating teapots, hold them with the handle in your right hand. This may sound strange, but the fact is that the vast majority of

An 'Up & Over' *Conical* milk and sugar in *Blue Chintz,* a *Daffodil* shape cup and saucer in *Nasturtium,* and a rare *Conical* covered sugar in *Honolulu.*

Clarice's all-over patterns had a front and back. *Melon* is orange-dominated on the front, while the reverse is primarily yellow. Only if the design is a motif repeated uniformly around the teapot will both sides look the same, such as on *Trees & House* or *Chintz*. With every piece being individually outlined, the way in which the design is placed on the teapot will also affect your estimation of its quality and therefore its value. If a key part of the design is too near the spout or the handle it should cost less.

A *Rooster* teapot from 1938 to 1939 (left) and a 1932 *Chick Cocoa* pot show the stylistic changes in Clarice's modelling during the Thirties.

One of Clarice's last modelled shapes, a *Celtic Harvest* teapot. It proved popular from 1937 until the war and also sold well afterwards.

The majority of Clarice's ware has colour banding, particularly the plates, saucers and teapot lids. Check that the banding colours are the same as those on the pattern, for occasionally sets were originally sold from stockists with the wrong saucers, having been mixed up when unpacked. And of course sets with a few missing pieces may have been 'made up' since. Sets with replacement pieces are still desirable, but this fact should be reflected in the price.

The saucers and plates of Clarice's teasets have impressed datemarks that were stamped on to them at the 'green clay' state, with the month number and year above a diamond shape. This pre-dates by months, or sometimes years, the actual date of decoration but gives collectors a definite clue as to the age of their pieces.

The condition of any collectable or antique must be taken into account when deciding if a price for a piece is fair. However, whereas one might be deterred from buying a damaged vase, with sets of teaware it is unwise

A selection of Clarice Cliff teacups: *Gardenia* on a rare *Devon* shape, a 1937 open-handled *Conical* teacup in *Taormina*, a mix of *Conical* and *Biarritz* cup and saucer in *Coral Firs* from 1935, and a traditional *Athens* shape in *Crocus* from 1931.

A *Lynton* shape *Early Morning set* in *Coral Firs* from 1935 to 1936.

to be so strict. Remember that the vast majority of Clarice's teapots were used for many years, and a small chip or crack will almost inevitably be found on a large set. Check carefully for fine hairlines, and be suspicious of 'bargains', which may have had the spout on the teapot completely restored. Ensure that you take off the lid of any teapot that interests you and peer into the pot. The more geometric of Clarice's shapes may have fine stress cracks, which can only be seen from the inside, and the underside of the lid may have sustained damage. Unless you can afford to be very choosy, these defects should not dissuade you from buying a well-painted set, but the seller should give a slight reduction in price.

Since *Bizarre* and *Fantasque* were hand-painted on-glaze, there may be surface scratches and wear in the paint on pieces in these designs. If these are very noticeable the piece is not a good investment, but ignore a few small scratches, as these give the piece 'age' and show that it was loved and used. If the teapot itself is in reasonable condition it is better to obtain an example than pass it by and wait many years before you have the chance to buy another.

Restoration is a word that strikes fear into all ceramic collectors. Good restoration can be nearly invisible, and the collector's best safeguard is to buy from credible dealers or auction houses. Ask if a piece is perfect, and you may save problems at a later date.

Christie's held the first All-Clarice Cliff sale in 1983, long before regular 'single designer' auctions were

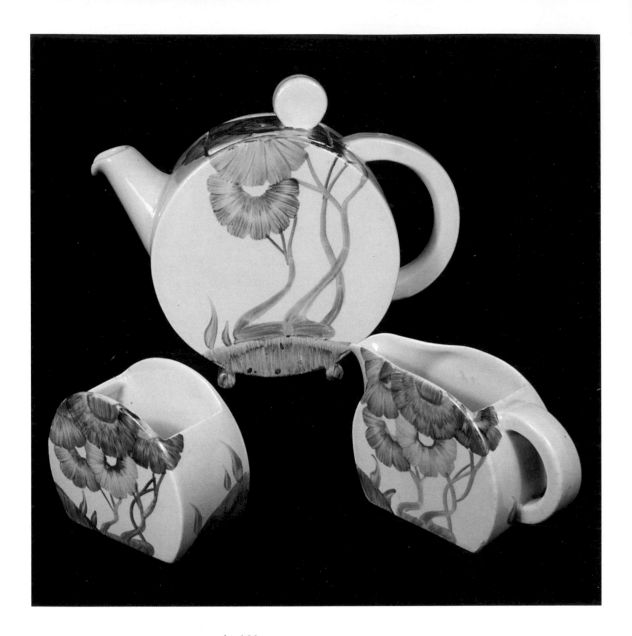

commonplace. It now holds two every year, and the viewings for these are an ideal opportunity to handle a real Clarice Cliff teapot. Christie's, South Kensington, has provided some typical prices for teapots and teasets on pp.104–111, but remember that something is actually worth what the *most* enthusiastic collector is prepared to pay for it.

Wedgwood has recently made good-quality reproductions of Clarice Cliff ware. The firm inherited the Newport and Wilkinson's sites from Midwinter, which became part of the group in the Eighties. The *Stamford* teapot, milk and sugar were accurately recreated in 1992 and 1993, and issued in *Pink Roof Cottage* and *Carpet*. These are already collectors' items and Wedgwood plans to reproduce further Clarice Cliff shapes and designs, so it is still possible to collect Clarice Cliff teapots on a budget.

It is hard to appreciate now how revolutionary Clarice's teaware shapes were when they first appeared. The twentieth century did not have a style of its own until Art Deco came along, as the roots of Art Nouveau went back to well before 1900. It is remarkable that it was to be an ordinary working-class girl called Clarice Cliff who first assimilated the new British industrial ceramics style. Modelling had been her previous priority, and the natural, flowing shapes she had been brought up with bore no relation to the angular, hard edges of Art Deco. However, having discovered colour, she then found form and – despite conflict with the factory's technical staff, who thought the shapes could not be

A *Bon Jour* shape trio in *Aurea*.

A traditional *Athens* shape teapot in *Rhodanthe,* with *Biarritz* plates in the same design in the background.

produced in earthenware – persisted and proved the sceptics wrong.

Clarice designed more tea and coffee shapes than any other industrial designer in the Thirties. She was also one of the first women to produce original teapots *en masse*. Paul Gibb of the Conwy Teapot Museum has observed, 'You will be hard-pressed to find an earlier lady teapot designer, unless there was someone who did but went uncredited!'

Clarice Cliff's achievements were great in number. Her teapots were unlike any ceramics seen before in Britain, with their shapes crying out for attention. Not only did she take ceramic design to a new level of technical intricacy, but her pieces were so effective that they spawned copies by virtually every company in Stoke. It is to her credit that few of these exhibit the same qualities as her originals. She changed public taste when she issued her *Conical* shapes in 1929, and designers at other factories had no choice but to emulate her. Even today the *Conical* tea-, coffeeware and vases look amazingly modern, and the numerous shapes that followed have such visual appeal that collectors value them very highly.

Most importantly, Clarice Cliff was the first British ceramic designer to understand and satiate the public demand for brash, all-over colour – something she was not scared to provide. Today's brightly coloured ceramics can be traced directly back to her. The extraordinary interaction between pure geometric shapes and bold rainbow-coloured patterns was the key to the success of *Bizarre by Clarice Cliff.*

Prices given here are original prices, where known, and (for comparison) current typical prices at auction, quoted in pounds sterling.

The Athens shape
1925–1937

A traditional shape with all pieces matching the set. Found in early designs, *Umbrellas & Rain*, and later ones such as *Rhodanthe*. Many *Athens* teapots were issued until 1937, but complete *Athens Early Morning sets* are rare.

A teapot in *Umbrellas & Rain* would have cost four shillings and two pence in 1930. This teapot would now cost £400 to £600.

The Bon Jour shape
1933–1941

Clarice's most mixed teaset used pieces from *Conical, Stamford* and *Biarritz* . Found in many 1933 to 1936 designs, including *Cowslip, Windbells, Honolulu, Idyll* and *Rhodanthe*. Later 1937 to 1940 examples are in simple banded designs or have a small floral motif.

A size 42 *Bon Jour* teapot in *Windbells* was six shillings in 1933. Value today £400 to £600. A complete *Early Morning set* in *Crocus* was fourteen shillings and three pence. It would now cost £700 to £1,200.

A *Lynton* shape teapot in *Honeydew* from 1935.

A *Conical* shape teapot in
Orange Roof Cottage from 1933
to 1934.

The Conical shape
1929–1937

Clarice's first geometric teaware has all matching shapes. In 1937 the triangular cup handles were 'open'.

This was Clarice's longest-lasting Art Deco shape so it is available in most of her designs, from *Trees & House* in 1930 to *Coral Firs* in 1935 A few rare *Appliqué* and *Latona* examples are known. It was made in all four sizes, as 42s, 36s, 30s and 24s.

A size 24 *Conical* teapot in an *Appliqué* design was eleven shillings. A size 42 in *Blue Firs* cost six shillings. The *Appliqué* would now be worth £1,000 to £3,000, the *Blue Firs* £800 to £1,200. *Conical Early Morning sets* vary from £600 to £4,000.

The Daffodil shape
1930–1936

All parts of the *Daffodil* teaware were custom-designed. Originally issued in a soft pink glaze called *Damask Rose*, then in floral designs such as *Crocus*. Various tableware designs are known, and occasionally *Fantasque* landscapes.

A size 30 *Daffodil* teapot in a *Fantasque* design was six shillings and nine pence in 1932. Cost today would be £400 to £1,000. A *Daffodil* teapot in *Damask Rose* would be £150 to £300.

The Eton shape
1930–1936

The *Eton* shape was limited to tea- and coffee-pots and a water jug.
The *Eton* shape is rare, so each

example listed may be unique. It is known in *Autumn, Solitude, Appliqué, Avignon, Lydiat, Blue Firs* and a few other designs. Theoretically it might be found in *any* design issued between 1930 and 1936.

Originally a teapot was six to seven shillings. Value now anything from £500 to £1,500. Few *Eton* teasets are known so there is no precedent for valuation, but they will be expensive.

The Globe shape
1925–1935

Every piece of the teaset was made for the *Globe* shape. Wilkinson's version of the traditional Staffordshire globe shape. Found in early 1928 designs like *Original Bizarre* and later ones such as *Gibraltar*. Many *Globe* teapots were sold until 1935.

Originally a teapot was four shillings. It would now cost £200 to £600. *Globe* shape *Early Morning sets*, although not Art Deco, sell well in strong designs such as *Gibraltar* and *Crocus*, from £500 to £1,200.

Le Bon Dieu shape
1932–1933

Surprisingly every piece of the teaset was custom-made for this shape.
The original decoration of this in 'bark and moss'-inspired colours is rare. The shape was then briefly issued in floral designs such as *Nasturtium*.

The original prices are not known. Regardless of decoration, a single piece would now be worth £100 to £200.

The Lynton shape
1934–1941

Every piece of the teaset was made for this shape.
Found only in later *Bizarre* designs such as *Rhodanthe* or *Coral Firs* and simple banded patterns. Many examples are in the unusual, but not valuable, *Goldstone* body.

Original prices not known. Teapots would now cost £50 to £600, complete sets £250 to £1,000, depending on design, but much less in *Goldstone*.

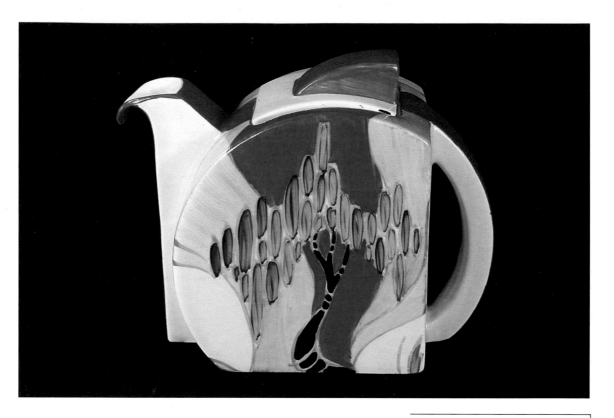

A *Stamford* shape *Fantasque Windbells* teapot from 1933.

The Stamford shape
1930–1936

All main pieces were designed for the shape, but *Conical* cups and saucers were used.

Very popular originally, so found in most designs issued between 1930 and 1936; frequently found in *Crocus, Autumn, Melon* or *Trees & House*. A few rare *Appliqué* or *Latona* examples are known.

A teapot was between six and nine shillings; cost now in a simple design £300 or for a rarity £2,000. A complete *Early Morning set* was fourteen shillings; now these start at £500 for simple designs and rise to £4,000+ for rarities.

The Trieste shape
1934–1937

All the pieces were designed for the shape except for cups, which were the *Conical*. Even the saucers were three-sided.

A stylish shape only produced in small quantities, seen in a few designs such as *Capri, Tartan, Forest Glen.*

Original prices unknown. Will now cost from £200 to £600 for a single teapot and £400 to £1,500 for a full *Early Morning set.*

The Circus teapot
1934–1936

A shape designed by Laura Knight under Clarice's supervision, in extremely limited quantities. Only two have been sold at Christie's Clarice Cliff auctions.

A single teapot costs £2,000 to £3,000, but there is no precedent for pricing a complete set.

Clarice's novelty teapots
1928–1939

These teapots confuse collectors. The 1928 *Bones the Butcher* was designed by Clarice Cliff but credited to Joan Shorter. *Bones the Butcher* was matched to a *Boy Blue* milk jug and *Humpty* sugar. The *Tee Pee* teapot credited to Clarice was designed by one of her girls, Betty Silvester.

Bones the Butcher was available between 1928 and 1933 but is now rare. Humorous and original, it would now cost £800 to £1,200. The *Tee Pee* teapot was designed for export to Canada before the war but was not issued until the Fifties and is more common, selling for £300 to £500. *Chick Cocoa* pots cost £200 to £400 and *Rooster* teapots a little less.

Other Clarice Cliff teapots
1932–1934

Marguerite and *My Garden* were issued with all parts of the teaset custom-designed.
The modelled teapot shapes with flower handles or knobs are not as collectable as Clarice's Art Deco teapots, but as such are more affordable, and still quite colourful.

The *Marguerite* and *My Garden* teaware can be found in several colourways and will cost £150 to £250 for a teapot.

Other Clarice Cliff teapots
1936–1939

Ironically, these later shapes all had most of the set custom-designed.

The modelled shapes that predominated during this time are less collectable. They often have a mushroom glaze finish rather than the honeyglaze but are still attractive and the cheapest way of owning a real Clarice Cliff teapot.

A *Raffia* teapot will be £100 to £150, a *Corncob* £75 to £100, and a *Celtic Harvest* £100 to £150. A *Windsor* will be £50 to £150, although in more colourful designs it may cost £150 to £250.

A 1930 to 1932 four-person *Conical* teapot in *Umbrellas,* with matching milk and sugar.

The teapot trail

Collections of teapots are found in surprising places, although Staffordshire, the home of the British teapot, is a good area in which to start looking.

- Hanley Museum in Stoke-on-Trent naturally has a wealth of teapots. It hopes to add Clarice Cliff examples soon. City Museum & Art Gallery, Hanley, Stoke-on-Trent ST1 3DW (01782 202173).
- Wedgwood has reproduced Clarice Cliff teapot shapes and displays Staffordshire teapots from the last three centuries at its museum at the Visitors' Centre, Barlaston, Stoke-on-Trent ST12 9ES (01782 204141).
- The Conwy Teapot Museum is housed in a medieval tower in North Wales. It has more than 1,000 'decorative arts' teapots. These date from 1700 to the Fifties, and include several rarities by Clarice Cliff. Open from Easter to October, the museum is at Paul Gibbs Antiques, 25 Castle Street, Conwy, Gwynedd L32 8AY (01492 593429).
- The Bramah Tea and Coffee Museum is the place to head for in London. It has the world's largest teapot, and a display of 1,000 tea- and coffee-pots, including some Clarice Cliff and Art Deco ones. They also sell *real* teas. The Clove Building, Maguire Street, London SE1 2NQ (0171 378 0222).

If you feel the urge to *buy* a real Clarice Cliff teapot, have a drink of strong tea, and go and see your bank manager first. Contact these specialist dealers, who often have some available:

- London: Banana Dance – Jonathan Daltrey (0181 699 7728)
- London: Markov & Beedles (0171 352 4545)
- Warwickshire: Rich Designs (01789 261612)
- Yorkshire: Art Deco Originals – Muir Hewitt (01422 347377)

Some of these dealers will be found at Art Deco Fairs, which take place on most weekends in various cities around Britain. They mean an early morning start to get the 'bargains', but give you the chance to inspect a number of pieces that you might not otherwise come across. Many of the dealers are fellow Clarice enthusiasts, so do ask them about their stock.

It takes a lot of courage to bid at auction, but you will inevitably be attracted to the All-Clarice Cliff auctions. Christie's, South Kensington (0171 581 7611) has held these annually since 1989. It now has spring and autumn sales, with 400–700 lots. Even if you do not bid, the fully illustrated catalogues are an inexpensive way to add to your knowledge of Clarice Cliff, and the viewing is a must. Bonham's, Knightsbridge (0171 393 3942) also now holds an All-Clarice Cliff auction every summer.

For the real devotee there is the Clarice Cliff Collectors Club. Founded in 1982, it has members around the world. The CCCC *Review,* issued three times a year, has articles about Clarice, *Bizarre*, archive material and auction news. Regional meetings are held, and at the annual Convention at Stoke-on-Trent members hear talks, see the archives and enjoy a reunion with Clarice's original *Bizarre* girls. For details, send an sae to: Subscriptions, CCCC, Fantasque House, Tennis Drive, The Park, Nottingham NG7 1AE.

Finally, you may just find that the teapot trail starts closer to home than you think. A visit to a relative who got married between 1928 and 1939 may reveal a Clarice Cliff teapot given as a wedding present. Or a look in the back of their cupboards may uncover an *Early Morning set* stored in a shoe-box. A few people are unknowingly still using their Clarice Cliff teapots to serve tea!

Thanks to those involved in the brew

The Conwy Teapot Museum, Hilary Bishop, John & Jean Broadbent, David & Barbara Gilfillan, David Latham, Sheila Murray, Shirley & Michael, Terry & Jo, Jonathan & Alan, Maureen & Harold, and other members of the Clarice Cliff Collectors Club, who provided teaware for photography.

The Hanley Reference Library, Stoke-on-Trent, for material from the Wilkinson's Archive.

The Clarice Cliff Collectors Club for archive pictures and excerpts from Clarice Cliff's letters (which may not be reproduced without written consent).

Christie's, South Kensington, which bravely priced the teapots.

Rene Dale, Eric Grindley, Edward Bramah, Jonathan Daltrey, Mike Slaney – without your ardent enthusiasm and support this book would not have been possible.

Doreen Jenkins, for her Darjeeling-strength proofreading and Earl Grey-quality observations on the manuscript.

'Clarice Cliff'® and 'Bizarre'™ are trademarks of Josiah Wedgwood & Sons Limited, Stoke-on-Trent, England, and are used with their permission.

Glossary

Bander & liner	a decorator who paints fine lines or thicker bands of colour on ware by applying the colour on a brush while rotating the ware on a potter's wheel
Boards	wooden planks (often six feet long) on which ware in various states of completion was carried between parts of the factory
Bottle-ovens	kilns built of brick, and fired by coal, which needed constant attention
Casting	pouring liquid clay (slip) into moulds in the shape of the ware, which dried out to form the piece in the 'green clay' state
Clay end	the area where clay was made into plates and bowls
Enamel kiln	a smaller oven used to fire ware with enamelled decoration on-glaze
Enameller	a decorator who applied colour either freehand or within another decorator's outline
Fancies	small, non-essential items, such as cauldrons, sabots, ink wells, bookends, which constituted an important part of *Bizarre* ware
Flat-pressers	an operative who used a steam-aided press to make saucers and plates from solid clay
Freehand	a decorator who applied a design with no existing guidelines, such as *Crocus* or *Tennis*
Gilding	painting fine gold lines on pottery
Glost warehouse	the storage area for glazed ware awaiting decoration. This was very

large on both the Newport and Wilkinson's sites, as Colley Shorter always believed in having a lot of ware in stock

Honeyglaze   Wilkinson's trade name for its clear glaze, which had 1 per cent iron oxide content, hence the name and colour

Kilns   smaller versions of bottle-ovens, where glazed or enamelled ware was fired

Matchings   ware to replace broken pieces of a set. One paintress specialized in these, as they had to match the style and colour of the original

Missus   a woman who supervised a decorating shop and trained the workers in the necessary techniques. The missus was generally an experienced paintress herself

On-glaze   decoration applied to the ware *after* it had been fired and glazed, which was then re-fired in the enamel kiln. This was the main style of decoration used on Clarice's hand-painted ware

Pochoir   a printing process popular in France, used to produce fine-quality prints in many colours

Potbank   the Staffordshire name given to a pottery, as in the early days they had a 'bank' of clay outside, and made 'pots'

The Potteries   a collective name for the six Staffordshire towns of Hanley, Tunstall, Longton, Burslem, Fenton and Stoke-on-Trent

Saggars   large earthenware boxes of diverse shapes to hold pottery during firing in the bottle-ovens and protect the ware from fumes

Shards   broken pieces of ware that formed white mounds – shard rucks – covering acres of land adjacent to the factories. In Staffordshire this is pronounced 'sherds'

Glossary

Stillages | open wooden shelves to hold boards, on which ware was carried from process to process in the factory

Under-glaze | ware decorated in the biscuit state before it was glazed – the traditional way of decorating printed ware, and rarely used for *Bizarre*

Bibliography

Clarice Cliff, Kay Johnson & Peter Wentworth-Shields, L'Odeon, 1976

Clarice Cliff – the Bizarre Affair, Leonard Griffin, Louis & Susan Pear Meisel, Thames & Hudson, 1988

The Rich Designs of Clarice Cliff, Richard Green, Des Jones & Leonard Griffin, Rich Publications, 1995

The Decorative Thirties, Martin Battersby, Studio Vista, 1969

Shelley Potteries, Watkins, Harvey, Senft, Barrie & Jenkins, 1980

The British Teapot, Janet & Tim Street-Porter, Angus & Robertson, 1981

The Shorter Connection, Irene & Gordon Hopwood, Richard Dennis Publications, 1992

Missuses and Mouldrunners, Jacqueline Sarsby, Open University Press, 1988

The Reviews of the Clarice Cliff Collectors Club, Leonard Griffin, CCCC, 1982–96

Clarice Cliff auction catalogues, Christie's, South Kensington, 1983–95

Thirties (exhibition catalogue), Arts Council, 1980